ZIPPY
AND THE
VERY BIG COOKIE

by Carla Golembe

In memory of my grandmother,
Gertrude Levowich

One rainy afternoon Zippy is hungry. He decides to *bake
a cake.

But Zippy does not know how to make a cake. And he only has
a *recipe for cookies.

Zippy does not want cookies. He wants a cake.
He decides to make one very big cookie. That will be just like
a cake.

Zippy puts eggs in a bowl.

He puts in butter.

He adds a cup of sugar.

He adds flour and chocolate *chips and mixes everything with a spoon.

He *pours it into a dish.

Zippy puts the dish in the *oven. His big cookie will be ready in forty minutes.

After ten minutes Zippy looks inside the oven. The cookie is getting bigger.

After twenty minutes the cookie smells good. The cookie is even
bigger now. It is taller than the dish.
"What a big cookie," says Zippy.

After thirty minutes when Zippy looks inside the oven, the cookie is so big he can't see the dish at all. "What a very big cookie!" says Zippy. "It's good I'm hungry."

14

After forty minutes Zippy is really hungry. He can't wait to eat his big cookie. But when he goes to take it out of the oven he cries, "Oh no!"
The very big cookie is pushing open the door of the oven.

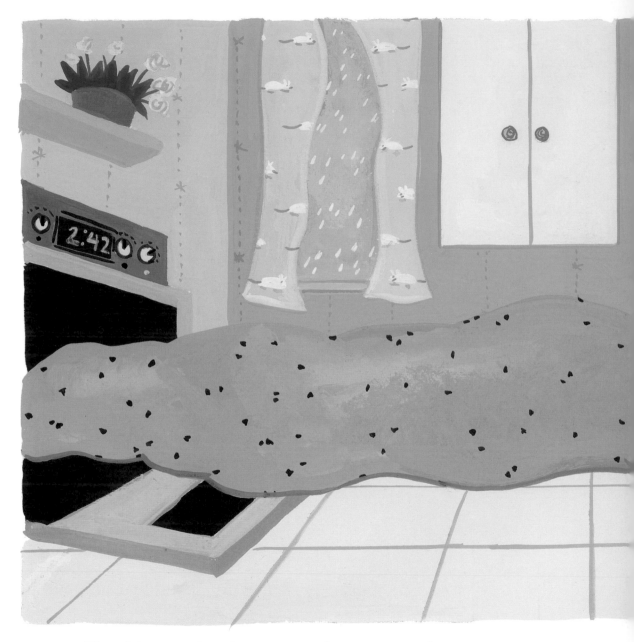

The big cookie keeps pushing. It pushes Zippy away
from the oven.

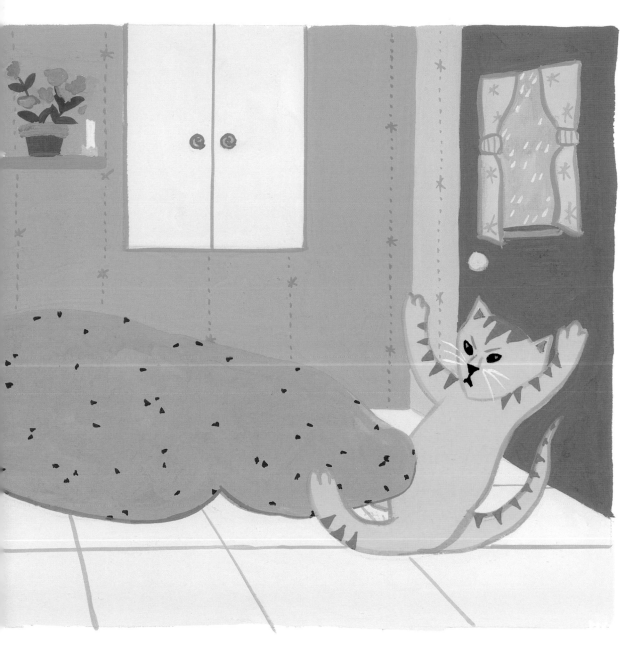

It pushes him *across the kitchen.

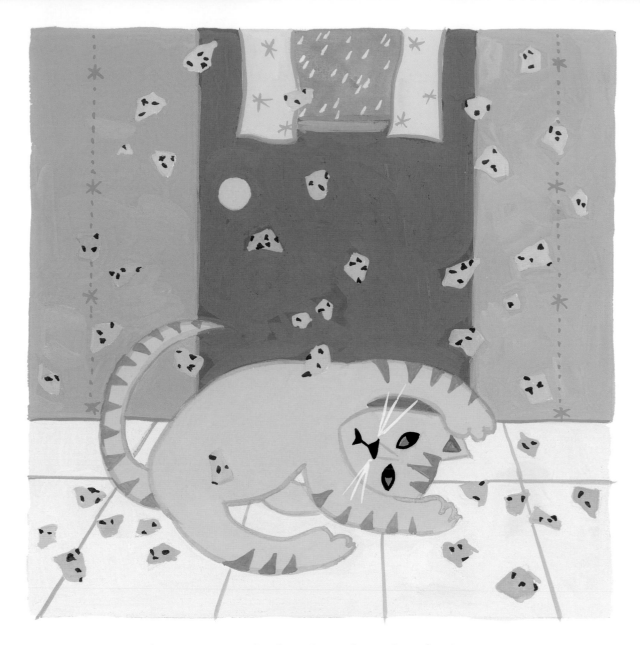

Then it *explodes in a hundred pieces.
"It's raining cookie!" *yells Zippy.

There is a knock on the door. It's Zoe. She looks at the pieces of the cookie and laughs and laughs.

Zoe tells Zippy, "There is a piece of cookie between your ears."

Zippy and Zoe eat all the pieces of the cookie.

"Now I'll teach you how to make a cake," says Zoe.

生字表

n.=名詞，prep.=介系詞，v.=動詞

賽ㄙㄞˋ皮ㄆㄧˊ與ㄩˇ超ㄔㄠ級ㄐㄧˊ大ㄉㄚˋ餅ㄅㄧㄥˇ乾ㄍㄢ

p.3

一ㄧˊ個ㄍㄜ下ㄒㄧㄚˋ雨ㄩˇ的ㄉㄜ午ㄨˇ後ㄏㄡˋ，賽ㄙㄞˋ皮ㄆㄧˊ肚ㄉㄨˋ子ㄗ餓ㄜˋ了ㄌㄜ，他ㄊㄚ決ㄐㄩㄝˊ定ㄉㄧㄥˋ烤ㄎㄠˇ個ㄍㄜ蛋ㄉㄢˋ糕ㄍㄠ來ㄌㄞˊ吃ㄔ。

p.4

但ㄉㄢˋ是ㄕˋ賽ㄙㄞˋ皮ㄆㄧˊ不ㄅㄨˊ會ㄏㄨㄟˋ做ㄗㄨㄛˋ蛋ㄉㄢˋ糕ㄍㄠ，而ㄦˊ且ㄑㄧㄝˇ，他ㄊㄚ只ㄓˇ有ㄧㄡˇ做ㄗㄨㄛˋ餅ㄅㄧㄥˇ乾ㄍㄢ的ㄉㄜ食ㄕˊ譜ㄆㄨˇ可ㄎㄜˇ以ㄧˇ看ㄎㄢˋ。

p.5

賽ㄙㄞˋ皮ㄆㄧˊ並ㄅㄧㄥˋ不ㄅㄨˋ想ㄒㄧㄤˇ吃ㄔ餅ㄅㄧㄥˇ乾ㄍㄢ，他ㄊㄚ想ㄒㄧㄤˇ吃ㄔ蛋ㄉㄢˋ糕ㄍㄠ，所ㄙㄨㄛˇ以ㄧˇ他ㄊㄚ決ㄐㄩㄝˊ定ㄉㄧㄥˋ做ㄗㄨㄛˋ一ㄧˊ個ㄍㄜ超ㄔㄠ級ㄐㄧˊ大ㄉㄚˋ餅ㄅㄧㄥˇ乾ㄍㄢ，大ㄉㄚˋ到ㄉㄠˋ像ㄒㄧㄤˋ一ㄧˊ個ㄍㄜ蛋ㄉㄢˋ糕ㄍㄠ一ㄧˊ樣ㄧㄤˋ。

p.6

賽ㄙㄞˋ皮ㄆㄧˊ在ㄗㄞˋ碗ㄨㄢˇ裡ㄌㄧˇ打ㄉㄚˇ了ㄌㄜ一ㄧˋ些ㄒㄧㄝ蛋ㄉㄢˋ。

p.7

又ㄧㄡˋ放ㄈㄤˋ了ㄌㄜ一ㄧˋ些ㄒㄧㄝ奶ㄋㄞˇ油ㄧㄡˊ。

p.8

再加上一杯糖。

p.9

然後他倒入麵粉和巧克力碎片，用湯匙把所有的東西攪拌在一起；

p.10

最後把它倒在烤盤上。

p.11

賽皮將烤盤放進烤箱裡烤。四十分鐘後，他的大餅乾就會完成了。

p.12

十分鐘過後，賽皮往烤箱裡看，發現那塊餅乾變大了。

p.13

二十分鐘過後，餅乾散發出香味，而且又變得更大了。它現在比烤盤還要高。
賽皮說:「這塊餅乾真大。」

p.14

三十分鐘過後，賽皮再往烤箱裡看，發現餅乾已經大到完全看不到下面的盤子了。
賽皮說：「這塊餅乾實在是很大！還好我肚子餓了。」

p.15

四十分鐘過後，賽皮真的好餓，他等不及要吃他的大餅乾了。
但是當他去把餅乾拿出烤箱時，他大叫：「喔，不！」
這塊超級大餅乾把烤箱的門擠開了！

p.16-17

大餅乾繼續膨脹推擠著，它把賽皮從烤箱推開，推到廚房的另一頭去了。

p.18

接著，它爆開變成上百個碎片！賽皮大叫：「下起餅乾雨來了！」

p.19

這時候有人敲門，原來柔依來了。她看到餅乾的碎片，笑個不停。

p.20

柔依告訴賽皮：「你兩隻耳朵中間有塊餅乾。」

p.21

賽皮和柔依吃掉了所有的餅乾碎片。

p.22

柔依說：「現在，我來教你怎麼做蛋糕吧！」

一一起く動ㄉㄨㄥ手ㄕㄡˇ做ㄗㄨㄛˋ菜ㄘㄞˋ單ㄉㄢ！

賽ㄙㄞˋ皮ㄆㄧˊ和ㄏㄜˊ柔ㄖㄡˊ伊ㄧ要ㄧㄠˋ邀ㄧㄠ請ㄑㄧㄥˇ好ㄏㄠˇ朋ㄆㄥˊ友ㄧㄡˇ們ㄇㄣ到ㄉㄠˋ家ㄐㄧㄚ裡ㄌㄧˇ吃ㄔ晚ㄨㄢˇ餐ㄘㄢ，但ㄉㄢˋ是ㄕˋ卻ㄑㄩㄝˋ不ㄅㄨˋ知ㄓ道ㄉㄠˋ要ㄧㄠˋ準ㄓㄨㄣˇ備ㄅㄟˋ什ㄕㄜˊ麼ㄇㄜ食ㄕˊ物ㄨˋ！小ㄒㄧㄠˇ朋ㄆㄥˊ友ㄧㄡˇ，一ㄧˋ起ㄑㄧˇ來ㄌㄞˊ動ㄉㄨㄥˋ動ㄉㄨㄥˋ腦ㄋㄠˇ，幫ㄅㄤ賽ㄙㄞˋ皮ㄆㄧˊ和ㄏㄜˊ柔ㄖㄡˊ伊ㄧ設ㄕㄜˋ計ㄐㄧˋ一ㄧˋ份ㄈㄣˋ好ㄏㄠˇ吃ㄔ又ㄧㄡˋ美ㄇㄟˇ觀ㄍㄨㄢ的ㄉㄜ菜ㄘㄞˋ單ㄉㄢ吧ㄅㄚ！

 第ㄉㄧˋ一ㄧˋ步ㄅㄨˋ：從ㄘㄨㄥˊ下ㄒㄧㄚˋ面ㄇㄧㄢˋ選ㄒㄩㄢˇ出ㄔㄨ你ㄋㄧˇ覺ㄐㄩㄝˊ得ㄉㄜ好ㄏㄠˇ吃ㄔ的ㄉㄜ食ㄕˊ物ㄨˋ，作ㄗㄨㄛˋ為ㄨㄟˋ你ㄋㄧˇ的ㄉㄜ菜ㄘㄞˋ單ㄉㄢ。

pea	**milk**	**rice**	**bread**
chicken	**fish**	**noodle**	**juice**
carrot	**egg**	**ham**	**coffee**

 第二步：一起來動手做！

準備一張圖畫紙和彩色筆或蠟筆，把你剛才選的食物寫上去，並畫上這些食物的樣子，這樣，你的菜單就大功告成了！

● 也可以在空白的地方畫上你喜歡的圖案，或是畫上可愛的賽皮和柔伊，讓你的菜單更獨一無二！

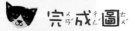 完成圖

Author's Note

This is based on a true story. When I was a little girl, my friends and I decided we wanted to bake one very big cookie. We mixed everything up, poured it into a cake pan and baked it. It exploded all over the oven.

作者的話

「賽皮與超級大餅乾」來自一個真實的故事。當我還是個小女孩時，我和我的朋友決定要烤一個超級大餅乾。我們把每樣東西都混合在一起，把它倒進一個裝蛋糕的盤子裡，然後拿去烤。結果它爆炸了，弄得整個烤箱都是。

🐾 About the Author

Carla Golembe is the illustrator of thirteen children's books, five of which she wrote. Carla has won several awards including a New York Times Best Illustrated Picture Book Award. She has also received illustration awards from Parents' Choice and the American Folklore Society. She has twenty-five years of college teaching experience and, for the last thirteen years, has given speaker presentations and workshops to elementary schools. She lives in Southeast Florida, with her husband Joe and her cats Zippy and Zoe.

🐾 關於作者

Carla Golembe 擔任過十三本童書的繪者，其中五本是由她寫作的。Carla 曾多次獲獎，包括《紐約時報》最佳圖畫書獎。她也曾獲全美父母首選基金會，以及美國民俗學會的插畫獎項。她有二十五年的大學教學經驗，而在過去的十三年中，曾經在多所小學中演講及舉辦研討會。她目前和丈夫Joe 以及她的貓——賽皮與柔依，住在美國佛羅里達州東南部。

賽皮與柔依系列

ZIPPY AND ZOE SERIES

想知道我們發生了什麼驚奇又爆笑的事嗎？
歡迎學習英文0-2年的小朋友一起來分享我們的故事 ——
「賽皮與柔依系列」，讓你在一連串有趣的事情中學英文！

精裝／附中英雙語朗讀CD／全套六本

Carla Golembe 著／繪

本局編輯部 譯

Hello！我是賽皮，我喜歡畫畫、做餅乾，還有跟柔依一起去海邊玩。偷偷告訴你們一個秘密：我在馬戲團表演過喔！

Hi，我是柔依，今年最開心的事，就是賽皮送我一張他親手畫的生日卡片！賽皮是我最要好的朋友，他很聰明也很可愛，我們兩個常常一起出去玩！

賽皮與柔依系列有：

1. 賽皮與綠色顏料
   (Zippy and the Green Paint)
2. 賽皮與馬戲團
   (Zippy and the Circus)
3. 賽皮與超級大餅乾
   (Zippy and the Very Big Cookie)
4. 賽皮做運動
   (Zippy Chooses a Sport)
5. 賽皮學認字
   (Zippy Reads)
6. 賽皮與柔依去海邊
   (Zippy and Zoe Go to the Beach)

國家圖書館出版品預行編目資料

Zippy and the Very Big Cookie:賽皮與超級大餅乾
/ Carla Golembe著;Carla Golembe繪;本局編輯
部譯.——初版一刷.——臺北市：三民，2006
　　面；　　公分.——(Fun心讀雙語叢書.賽皮與柔
　　依系列)
中英對照
ISBN 957–14–4452–9　　(精裝)
1.英國語言－讀本
523.38　　　　　　　　　　　　　　94026566

網路書店位址　http://www.sanmin.com.tw

© Zippy and the Very Big Cookie
—— 賽皮與超級大餅乾

著作人　Carla Golembe
繪　　書　Carla Golembe
譯　　者　本局編輯部
發行人　劉振強
著作財
產權人　三民書局股份有限公司
　　　　臺北市復興北路386號
發行所　三民書局股份有限公司
　　　　地址／臺北市復興北路386號
　　　　電話／(02)25006600
　　　　郵撥／0009998–5
印刷所　三民書局股份有限公司
門市部　復北店／臺北市復興北路386號
　　　　重南店／臺北市重慶南路一段61號
初版一刷　2006年1月
編　　號　S 806191
定　　價　新臺幣壹佰捌拾元整
行政院新聞局登記證局版臺業字第○二○○號

ISBN　957–14–4452–9　　(精裝)